ICT COURSEWORK
FOR A2 LEVEL

BARBARA WILSON

Hodder Murray

A MEMBER OF THE HODDER HEADLINE GROUP

Orders: please contact Bookpoint Ltd, 130 Milton Park, Abingdon, Oxon OX14 4SB.
Telephone: (44) 01235 827720. Fax: (44) 01235 400454. Lines are open from 9.00 – 5.00,
Monday to Saturday, with a 24 hour message answering service.
You can also order through our website www.hoddereducation.co.uk.

British Library Cataloguing in Publication Data
A catalogue record for this title is available from the British Library

ISBN 10: 0 340 87175 X
ISBN 13: 978 0 340 87175 1

First Published 2003
Impression number   10 9 8 7 6 5
Year   2009 2008 2007

Copyright © 2003 Barbara Wilson

Typeset by Dorchester Typesetting Group Ltd
Printed in Great Britain for Hodder Murray, a member of the Hodder Headline Group,
an Hachette Livre UK Company, 338 Euston Road, London NW1 3BH by CPI, Antony Rowe

Contents

Introduction and what makes an A2 project

This book is intended to help with A2 level project work in ICT. Like the book in the same series on AS project work, it does not contain a whole sample project or seek to say 'this is exactly what you have to do', but gives guidance on how to approach project work and provides ideas for techniques to use.

For many people ICT projects at this level will be the hardest piece of project work they have ever attempted and also the biggest in terms of volume and complexity. As with all problems, they become more manageable if broken down into smaller parts and the book is arranged with this in mind.

In all of the work that you do, it is important to remember just what ICT is about. It is simply the use of technology to input, store, process, transfer and output information. So every project must be concerned with these things. Different businesses and individuals do these tasks in different ways but everything comes down to these five stages, no matter how complex it seems to begin with.

So why do you have to do project work?

The answer is simple, to test your ability to use the knowledge that you have gained through theory work and apply it in a real or realistic situation. It also allows you to learn skills and techniques that cannot be taught through theory work alone.

When your project work is assessed the marker is not just looking at your skill with one or more software packages, but in your ability to provide an ICT solution to a problem – something that involves a whole range of skills. This is why the projects are assessed over a range of criteria and categories from analysis to evaluation.

Planning out your work, keeping to deadlines set and organising yourself are important 'life' skills and all of these are needed to complete the project successfully. More marks are probably lost through not completing sections, for example design work, than through an inability to do the work.

A2 level projects involve producing a **reusable system** for a **real** end user. This means that you are looking at a bigger problem than for AS and producing more than a 'one-off' solution. The solution produced must be reusable over time and may be capable of producing 'management style' information. The A2 level project must be produced using a 'Systems Development Life Cycle' approach and involves the use of more advanced techniques and skills than for AS projects. It also builds on what has been learnt from an AS project.

All project work in ICT is attempting to encourage you into what has become in many cases best practice in the industry. You may not be aware but over the years many problems have been caused by solutions that have simply been created by programmers to do what they *think* the end user wants. Often this was not what the end user actually did want and so the business failed to benefit. Many solutions have been badly documented. This leads to tremendous problems when a program needs updating, a member of staff leaves or something needs to be added to the program. For example, lack of documentation and forward planning led to many companies spending large sums of money trying to cure 'Millennium' problems and adjusting programs to cope with the euro.

Project work should be a challenge, it should be fun and also it should keep you interested and busy. There is a real feeling of satisfaction from providing a solution to someone's problem that does what it is supposed to do. It will not always go smoothly, you will have problems, you will get fed up and frustrated but this can happen when you do anything challenging. You will learn a lot, not just in terms of ICT but in how to go about solving problems, communicating with people, being self critical (very important in ICT), helping others and in producing a detailed piece of work to a high standard that you can be proud of. Many students use their project work when going for jobs or as the basis of project work needed for higher level courses. So enjoy and learn.

What is different about A2 projects?

An A2 project is not just another AS project. The requirements of an A2 project are designed to test a different set of skills as well as reinforce ones that have already been learnt.

As you are another year older, and hopefully wiser, more is expected of you. You are expected to be able to deal with more complex problems, so the projects should be based on a system, rather than a task.

In the theory modules of your course you will be learning about more complex issues, for example not just about *what* makes a good user interface but *why* it does – how people actually relate to Information Technology Systems.

So what is the difference between a system and a task? The simple answer is that a system is bigger and more complex and contains several tasks!

Here is an example:

For an AS project a student has produced a solution that allows a landscape gardening company to fulfil the task of producing accurate, well presented quotations.

An A2 project might be a system from which the owner of the landscaping company can gain information to help them develop the business. It would be a system that can be reused over time and is not just a one-off

solution. It could perhaps:

- keep a record of quotes produced
- enable the owner to see how long it takes people to respond to the quotes
- see how many people who have quotes actually decide to get the work done
- compare the price quoted with the actual invoice value for the work
- record and keep track of payments
- allow analysis of customers, success or otherwise of advertising, trends in the business over time e.g. seasonally or yearly

In general, it should provide information on which decisions can be made about the business and allow the owner to plan and organise the business, not just once, but over a period of time.

Here are some dos and don'ts when choosing possible A2 projects:

Do

- Have a real end user – this is essential for success in an A2 project and is usually a specific requirement of the exam board.
- Make sure you will be able to keep in contact with your end user and discuss things with them as the project progresses.
- Look for a business or area that you are interested in – you will be spending a long time working on the project so you need to be interested in it.
- Choose an area that will give you sufficient scope to demonstrate your skills, but that isn't too complex.
- Make sure that it is a system, not a task.
- Make sure that you will be able to produce 'management information' from the system, that it isn't just what some people call an 'electronic pin board'.
- Be aware that you should be able to consider changes over time.

Don't

- Try to be your own end user or use a fellow student as your end user unless there is a good reason to do so.
- Make up a situation.
- Take on something that is too big for a project – take your teacher's advice, much better to be able to complete all the sections in time than have a half finished project. It is easier to add things on to a simpler problem.
- Do what you did for your AS project using a different piece of software.
- Just do what you did for your AS project and make it 'bigger'.

Note

It is actually against exam board rules to submit the same work for more than one module. If you are found doing this it can lead to severe penalties.

There are lots of possibilities for projects. Sometimes students have produced systems for new businesses or new systems for an existing business that allow the business to move into different areas. An example here might be a shop that decides to start doing home deliveries, or a joiner who wants to get into kitchen designs.

In general one area not to select is a website. A website could be part of an A2 project if it is used for output from the system itself. It is difficult to use a website for input to a system if you are doing an ICT project given current software as this involves programming in a programming language which is not considered to be a skill for ICT.

Most presentation type software packages are not on their own suitable to use for A2 projects and the majority of ICT students tend to base their A2 projects on either Relational Database Management Software or Spreadsheet Software.

Perhaps the most important consideration when choosing your project area is that you will be able to analyse the existing or proposed system thoroughly as this is where there are a lot more marks given and a lot more detailed work needed to be done than in an AS project.

Example of comparison in mark allocations for AS and A2

The following table shows a comparison of the requirements for Modules 3 and 6.

MODULE 3			MODULE 6		
Specification	13	22%	Analysis	18	20%
			Design	16	18%
Implementation	20	33%	Implementation	15	17%
Testing	12	20%	Testing	15	17%
Evaluation	6	10%	Evaluation	10	11%
User documentation	9	15%	User guide	8	9%
			Report	8	9%
Total	**60**	**100%**	**Total**	**90**	**100%**

If you look at the table above, you can see that for an A2 project 38% of the mark is awarded to analysis and design compared to just 22% to the specification in an AS project. Only 17% of the mark is awarded to implementation and 17% to testing, compared to 33% and 20% in the AS.

The reason is that different skills are being tested in each project. So what does it mean for you?

It means that you must not expect to complete your analysis and design work in a week or two and then be able to spend two to three months on the implementation! You have got to spend more time at the start of this project.

At AS you may have seen that attention to detail, making sure that you understand what inputs, processes and outputs are required and what the end user needs, are critical to the success of an AS project. The same is true for an A2 project. The difference is that whereas before you probably fairly quickly had a good idea of what was involved, with a more complex problem and a system rather than a task, you have to move towards using what are described as 'formal methods' for analysis as there is a lot more to think about and plan for. Without using some sort of organised approach you will simply get in a muddle or start working on something that isn't going to work or do what the end user wants and you will end up wasting a lot of time.

Chapter

1.

What are formal methods and why are they used?

My experience of students has shown that very few actually understand why formal analysis is needed when they start on their project work, but by the end of it they have learned what goes wrong if you don't do it!

A little history may help. Computers haven't been around for very long but the development and spread of their use has happened very rapidly. After the Second World War their use in the field of commerce took off. But there were no ready-made programmers at that time, people were learning the technical skills as they went along and those who were interested became the first programmers. These people were interested in the 'art' of programming and took pleasure from getting programs to work and using sophisticated techniques – much like those of you who enjoy programming now.

The only problem with this was that these programmers didn't necessarily have a lot of knowledge of the business they were working for and they often didn't bother, have the skills, or have time, to find out much about what the people or departments who would use the programs actually wanted. This was where the job of the systems analyst first emerged – their job was to discover what was needed and to translate it into what could be done in computing terms so that the programmers could then write and test the programs to solve the problem.

Again the people who moved into the roles of analysts tended to be those who were good at programming and wanted promotion. Unfortunately the skills needed to be a good programmer don't always make a good analyst! Talking to a computer is a bit different to talking to an end user!

Also most of the early systems that were automated were simple data processing systems where the actual problem was not very complex, there were just large volumes of work to be processed. All of this meant that basic solutions of some sort could be produced that did the job.

As systems became more complex and users more demanding, the analysts found it more and more difficult to keep track of what was required and pass on the right information to the programmers. This meant that users were not getting what they wanted and companies started to question just what they were getting for their money.

Other problems like rapid staff turnover meant that there was a need to document all of the work from an early stage so that other people could complete a project, project teams were needed and some sort of common way of communicating was needed. It soon became obvious that if you didn't understand what the end user wanted and how the current system operated, you were never going to be able to produce a solution that did what was required!

The answer came from engineering, where rigorous methods of specifying, designing, implementing and testing products had been in use for some time – this is where the term 'software engineering' comes from.

Over a fairly short period of time several different methods for controlling and structuring the way an IT system was produced were developed and these soon became essential to the process of efficiently and effectively producing IT solutions to business problems. They took off quickly because there was an obvious need for them and large corporations developed their own in-house standards based on the basic methods that had been put forward.

These are the **formal methods** that you need to use in your own analysis work to prevent you having the problems that used to occur, and to some extent still occur in industry today. There really is nothing more frustrating than spending hours slaving over a hot computer to end up with what you think is a good solution only to find your user not bothering to use the solution!

What do formal methods do?

They give you a structure to help you break down complex problems and document them in a way that makes it easy to discuss with your end user and then to refine and develop your solution. In theory modules you will be covering the formal systems development life cycle and should come across the ideas discussed here.

No one is saying this type of work is easy, it isn't, and it is why analysts have traditionally been paid a lot more than programmers! But if you understand what the methods are trying to achieve it is worth persevering because they really do make the subsequent stages of the project work a lot easier.

Don't feel disheartened if you find using the techniques described in the next chapters difficult – everyone does when they first try using them and by that I mean experts as well as students! Understanding complex problems is never easy and usually the biggest problems are caused by not knowing enough to begin with or not getting enough answers to questions before you start, so make sure that the investigation of the current system is carried out thoroughly. Don't ever be afraid of asking questions. If you don't have the answers the work is much harder as you end up imaging that you know how something works and when you don't, that's when problems occur.

Getting started on your major project

In the AS book techniques that could be used to find out about your business were discussed. The most popular method of finding out information for your AS project was probably to conduct an interview with the proposed end user. This is not, however, the easiest thing to do. Some of the points to consider before such an interview were given in the AS book as:

1 Always prepare for an interview. Can you find any information out about the business in advance?

2 Who is the end user? Is there just one person or are there several? Will they all want to do the same things?

3 How are you going to arrange the interview? Will you write a letter to ask them to see you and arrange a date and time? This can be useful as you can send a copy of the questions that you want to ask in advance to give people time to consider them beforehand.

4 A copy of any letter sent and even better, the reply received can be put into your project. If you use emails to set up or conduct a meeting then include copies of these.

5 Always be polite and explain why you need the persons help and how important it is for your exam work.

6 What questions are you going to ask? You must plan these out beforehand.

7 Don't have too many questions. You will probably only need to ask about ten. Any more and you will be taking up too time and also get too much information at once.

8 Think about how you are going to record your answers to the questions. Having the questions on one piece of paper and putting the answers on another can be difficult if you are just sat on a chair and trying to juggle everything around. It is better to use just one piece of paper and leave spaces to put the answers in.

9 Another idea is to use a Dictaphone or tape recording device of some type. If you can get one of these it is useful as often it is hard to remember everything that has been said or write it down and manage to concentrate at the same time. If you do this ask permission from the person you are interviewing first.

10 Always write up the results of an interview straight away afterwards before you forget what the notes you made meant.

11 It is useful, and polite, to send a copy of your write up of the interview to the interviewee and ask them to sign it as a true record of the interview. This has several advantages – you can get confirmation that what you have written is correct, it gives you the chance to include any questions that you forgot to ask or now realise you need the anwers to, and it gives you more evidence to go in your

project. You also know that you are working with correct facts rather than your interpretation of what was said.

12 Ask if you can have copies of any documents used by the business. Things like invoices, quotes, membership application forms, appointment cards, customer records and so on. These could be blank or preferably contain data.

Remember there are various other important ways of finding out more about your organisation, which you will have used for your AS project.

Think about how successful you were at finding out information for your first project using interviews and other methods and how you could have improved the way you went about it. Because your AS project was a much simpler problem it would have been a lot easier to do. Now you are looking at a system and the demands on it over time.

The existing system

This means how the business functions at the moment. In other words how the end user's requirements are met now. The existing system may be purely manual, it could be partly or fully automated, or it may not even exist except for in an end user's mind! This is the case where you may be asked to produce a system for a new business function. Whichever it is, it needs to be analysed. But what needs to be analysed and just what is analysis?

Analysis is the process of breaking down a complex real life system into its component parts – modelling the real world. So what you are going to be producing is a model. Design is the opposite – it involves taking the model and producing a real working solution – going back to the real world!

In ICT and computing we are concerned with information so what you have got to start by modelling is the **information flows and data dynamics of the existing system**.

Put simply this means that you have got to find out about:

- inputs and their sources
- processes
- data stores
- data flows between processes, stores, sources and destinations
- outputs and their destinations
- the boundary of the system

As you will probably have had to do the same sort of thing for your first project, you should be able to understand what these mean. If you don't, read on and see if it becomes clearer.

Note

The reason many students steer away from presentation-style projects for A2 is that actually modelling the processes involved is very difficult as the processes are generally mental ones, which are the hardest to deal with. I certainly do not recommend students to go for that type of project without warning them of the consequences first – which are that they will find it much harder to gain good marks on the analysis!

2

Breaking the problem down

As mentioned in the last chapter you have got to be able to identify data and processes in the system that exists at the moment before you can start to design any alternative system. This is what makes sure that you understand what is going on. This is the stage of modelling or going from the real world to the theoretical world – probably the hardest bit of the lot to do!

To make it easier the best way to start is by working out what goes on – in other words what are the processes involved in the system you have chosen?

Note

But be careful – don't start doing your implementations yet. This is probably the silliest mistake that students make. You really don't know enough yet. You may think that you do but experience shows this is not true. I have had more problems with students who have rushed ahead and started to build their systems than I have had with students who spend longer on the analysis. So don't start to implement at the same time as analysing the system!

Decomposition

Decomposition is a good starting point as it deals solely with the processes involved in a system, no data flows or data stores are considered at this point. It answers the question 'What does the system you are studying, actually **do**?'

The principal of decomposition is that you start by identifying what are called the **high level processes** within a system and then gradually break them down into sub-processes until they can be broken down no further and you have the **elementary processes** in the system. An example is shown in figure 2.1.

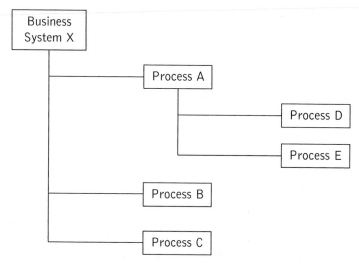

Figure 2.1 Basic decomposition diagram.

Here the business system is identified as business system X. The high level processes are processes A, B and C and then process A is broken down into two further sub-processes D and E. Processes B, C, D and E are all elementary processes as they cannot be broken down further.

Figure 2.2 illustrates an example of decomposition used for a stock system. Notice that each process has a verb (or doing word) to describe it – if you can't put one in the label then it isn't a process. If you want to say 'does this **and** that' then it is not an elementary process.

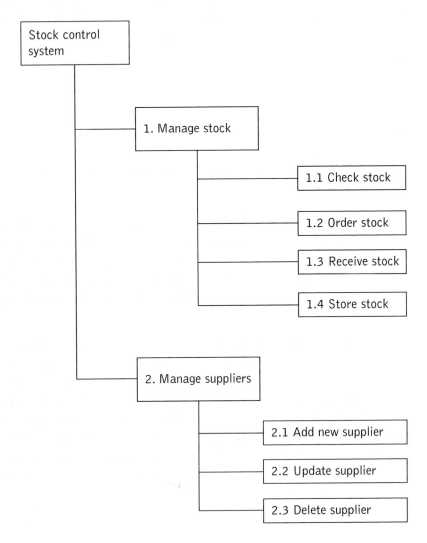

Figure 2.2 Decomposition diagram used for a stock system.

In this example there are only two high level processes – manage stock and manage suppliers. The system has two levels shown. This is indicated by the numbering used above – this starts to give a logical structure to the project work and can be used later in your project. It also means it doesn't matter what you call the individual processes as you have labels to refer to them by. You will be describing what each one involves in detail later on. In fact there are very few words that get used to describe processes involving data. Common ones include:

- add
- amend
- delete
- sort
- search/find
- update
- produce

If you have difficulty in knowing what to put down it is usually not because you are stupid, but because you have not found out enough from your end user about the system. You might not have spent enough time observing or asking the right questions, which is why you need to understand the importance of, and the best ways of, interviewing and getting information from your end user.

The benefit of starting with this technique is that it is simple. It allows you to see just how big the system is that you are intending to use. As a rough guide, I would suggest that anything containing more than four high level processes or needing to be decomposed to more than three levels is too complex for a project at this level. It may be necessary to concentrate on just some of the processes involved i.e. a sub-system. This is one of the advantages behind analysing the existing system and then making proposals for a new system where you can set the boundary of the system at a sensible size for a project.

Once you have something down on paper you can then discuss your ideas with your teacher and see if they think that it is a sensible size and offers the scope for you personally to manage.

This type of diagram shows that you understand that you are looking at a system and not just a series of isolated tasks, so don't be tempted to draw different ones for different bits of the system you are looking at.

Some rules for drawing up decomposition diagrams are given overleaf but generally I have found that you do not have to worry too much about these rules and it should be noted that time is generally not considered within data flow diagrams.

Note

Be careful not to do everything on the computer. When you start trying to draw decomposition diagrams and, later on, data flow diagrams, you end up constantly changing them. A good supply of paper and pencils are most useful. It also means that this is all work that you can get on with without having to have access to a computer. You can always produce a neat copy or a copy in a word-processed document when you know that you have got it right.

Basic rules for decomposition

1 A process, which is decomposed, must consist of two or more processes. For example:

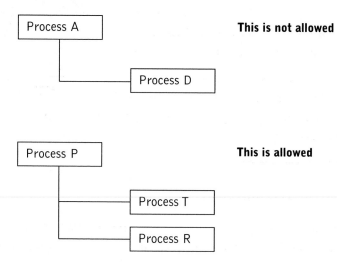

| Process A | **This is not allowed** |

| Process D |

| Process P | **This is allowed** |

| Process T |

| Process R |

2 A process must be completely defined by the sub-processes of which it is composed.

3 Decomposition of processes should start at the highest level and work down (top-down approach) until the elementary processes have been found.

4 An elementary process has the characteristics that:

  i it is triggered by the arrival of an input, the completion of another elementary process or by a specific time being reached,

  ii once started, a process will continue executing until it is complete without having to wait for any other process or the arrival of other data,

  iii it has no sub-processes that can be executed independently.

Examples of i would be where:

• the entering of sales details prompts the production of an invoice,

• the 31st March being reached results in the production of an annual report,

• once an application form is received a new member's details are entered.

Hill House Stables, an example description of a business

This chapter uses a case study based on a livery stables for horses. Many of you will probably not be familiar with one of these and will wonder what it is all about! It is used here as a case study for this very reason – the more familiar you are with a system, the less you bother to find out about it, as you think you know the answers. The result is that your analysis work is poor. If there is anything that you don't understand you can always use a dictionary – you will probably come across unfamiliar words in any project that you do – but I would be surprised if there is: remember, you are concerned with information systems, not physical systems. So, read on . . .

Mrs Rayner runs a livery stables and bed and breakfast in a village in Cheshire. The business involves Mrs Rayner looking after horses for people. This means that she has to feed them, provide grazing for them, organise shoeing and injections or other vet's visits and sometimes provide extra services like exercising and clipping.

There are currently over 50 horses and ponies at the stables owned by 40 different owners. Mrs Rayner would like to be able to expand the numbers to approximately 100 horses and ponies and, theoretically, each of these could belong to a different owner although in practice there always tend to be some owners who have more than one horse.

Mrs Rayner employs several full and part time staff to care for the horses. Her main assistant, Sarah, has day-to-day responsibility for all of the horses and she and Mrs Rayner discuss the work that needs doing on a regular basis.

Some owners have been with Mrs Rayner since she started the business but others come and go. There is probably a turnover of around 10 owners per year as children lose interest in their ponies or people leave the area and new clients join the stables.

The owners have to be adults so in some cases it is necessary for Mrs Rayner to keep details of the children who actually ride the ponies as well as the parents who own them.

When a client brings a horse to Hill House, Mrs Rayner has to record all the details she needs on a record card which she keeps in a small card file. On one side of the

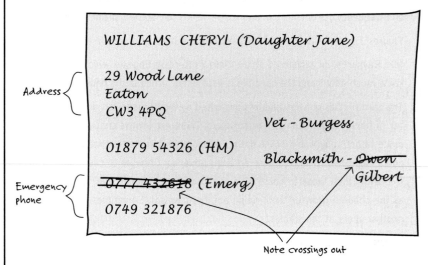

Figure 3.1a Index Card Hill House Side One – Client Details.

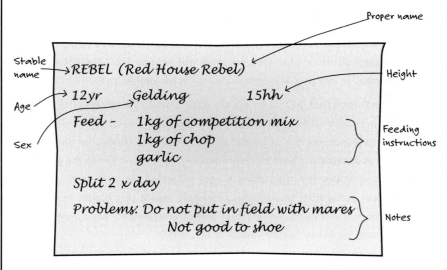

Figure 3.1b Index Card Hill House Side Two – Horse/Pony Details.

card she records the name and address of the owners and if needed the children's names, a home and work telephone number or an alternative emergency number. Also on this side she records the name of the vet and blacksmith used by the client.

On the reverse of the card she notes down the details about the horses/ponies owned. This information includes: name (including stable name), age, sex, feed (type, amount and frequency), problems e.g. aggressive, needs hay soaked, prone to laminitis etc.

Figures 3.1 shows an example of the front and back of a card in the card file.

Mrs Rayner is not registered on the Data Protection Register which she didn't really know much about and the card file is kept in her office in the house.

The card file has got less and less organised as the business has grown and the number of horses at the stables has increased. There are always changes that need to be made to both client and horse data. For example if someone changes jobs and telephone number or decides to use an alternative vet. Changes to client data occur less frequently than those to horse data as many clients change their horses and ponies as the children grow or their riding ability increases. Sometimes a horse is sold to another client at the stables.

Mrs Rayner allows clients to choose their own blacksmiths and vets. The clients sign a form giving the vet's details and stating that they will allow Mrs Rayner to call the vet if needed in an emergency. These forms are kept in the staff room in the stable yard, which is kept locked when no one is around. They are filed alphabetically by name of client.

Figure 3.2 shows an example of the form that is used.

Mrs Rayner also needs to keep the name of the blacksmith used on the record card. She keeps the names of all the blacksmiths and vets and their telephone numbers and addresses as well as a note of their charges in her address book.

Sarah keeps a book, a large page-a-day diary, in which she records all of the chargeable work done each day for each horse. Mrs Rayner needs this when she and Sarah have to prepare the bills at the end of each month. The charges for livery and other services are kept in a word processed document that is printed out and given to each client when they join the stables. A copy is kept on the staff room notice board. Invoices are written by hand on a two-part invoice pad bought from the local stationers. The invoices are posted to owners who generally pay by cheque or cash and hand the money to either Sarah or Mrs Rayner.

Figures 3.3 and 3.4 show examples of a price list and sample invoice for Hill House Stables.

HILL HOUSE LIVERY STABLES

LIVERY AGREEMENT

Name of Client: ....

Address: ....

....

Telephone Number: ....

Name of horse/pony: ....

Sex: .... Colour: ....

Age: .... Height: ....

Any allergies/special conditions we should know about: ....

....

....

....

Feed: AM: .... PM: ....

....

....

....

....

....

Name of veterinary surgeon: ....

Telephone number: ....

Name of farrier: ....

Telephone number: ....

Insurance company: ....

Type of livery: ....

Monthly rate: ....

Terms: ....

....

....

....

Figure 3.2 Form used to record vet and blacksmith details.

Hill House Stables

<u>LIVERY PRICE LIST</u>
1st September 2002

		Per Week	Per Month
Full Livery –	Exceeding 16.2 hh	£75	£325.00
	Exceeding 15.2 hh	£70	£303.33
	Exceeding 14.2 hh	£65	£281.66
	Under 14.2 hh	£60	£260.00

All prices are based on straw bedding, and does not include exercise

	Shavings Supplement	£5 per week	
	Carrots	Shared Cost	

DIY Livery –	Stable & Grazing	£20	£86.66
	Feed & Turnout – No Rugs	£1 per time	
	Feed & Turnout with rugs	£2.50	
	Feed, turnout & muck out	£7.50	
	Day livery (AM & PM stable duties)	£10	
	Bring In & Finish (PM)	£2.50	

<u>LIVERY EXTRAS</u>

Exercise	£5-£10 per session
Clipping	£15-£25
Trimming	£5-£10
Plaiting	£5
Wormers	£10-12
Lessons	£15

Figure 3.3 Print out of livery price list.

Hill House Stables

INVOICE

Date: *01 Sept 02*

SERVICE RENDERED	DATE	PRICE
Stable & Grazing	*Sept*	*86.66*
Muck out & Turn out 7 days @ £7.50		*52.50*
All day care 15 days @ £10/day		*150.00*
Exercise 7 times @ £5 time		*35.00*
1 Wormer		*10.00*
7 Bales of Straw £1.75p/bale		*12.25*
Bring in x 2 @ £1		*2.00*
	TOTAL DUE	*348.41*

Figure 3.4

Business problems

These include:

- An expanding business meaning more paperwork.
- As the business grows more staff are needed and the need to communicate information to other people increases.

- Time spent on paperwork reduces the time available for actually working outside and means extra staff are needed. For example the paperwork currently takes Mrs Rayner at least 20 to 30 hours per month and she pays her staff £5 per hour so it is costing her a minimum of £100 to £150 to do the paperwork.
- As she is always rushing around, mistakes get made and bills are added up incorrectly – this leads to clients getting annoyed and can result in lost business.
- Sometimes Sarah forgets what she has done for a horse and so the charges get left off the bill and as a result Mrs Rayner loses money.
- Time is wasted in writing out lists and telling the staff verbally what is required.
- Poor presentation gives a bad image to the business.
- Staff sometimes misunderstand or get confused by scribbled notes and this results in wasted time and can cause more serious problems. For example, horses that don't get on may be put in the same field.

The result is that the business is limited in its size and unless something is improved Mrs Rayner will be unable to continue as rising business rates and interest charges mean that unless she can increase her income she will fail to make sufficient money to cover her costs.

Looking at the system

Notice that in any description of a business there will be information that you don't need, as well as things that you will have missed when you first investigate, so it is a good idea to make clear which aspects of the business you are going to concentrate on.

The area I am going to concentrate on is record keeping and preparing invoices.

How records are kept and invoices prepared

To find out the details for this I spent several days at the stables during which I watched Sarah and Mrs Rayner, including watching the bills being prepared, and interviewed both of them. While I was watching I made notes and then got copies of the documents that they used.

Records

When a new client's horse arrives   Mrs Rayner gets a new card from the pile that she keeps in her desk drawer. She then fills in the details for the client on one side of the card, and for the horse on the other side of the card. They then look something like Figure 3.1.

She also gets the owner to fill in the vet's form. If the vet or blacksmith are different from ones that other clients use she will check in her address book whether she has their details and if not adds them to her lists.

She gives a copy of the charges sheet that she has printed out to the owner.

When the forms are completed she adds the card to her card file, which is filed in alphabetical order of owner. The vet form is taken to the staff room in the yard and filed with the others in alphabetical horse name order in the A4 file.

When a client's details need changing   Mrs Rayner is usually told either in person or by phone of any changes to telephone numbers, addresses or horse details. She will find the card in the file, cross out old details and add new ones in.

When a client leaves   Mrs Rayner hasn't so far had much changeover of clients as the business has not been going very long. At present all she does is once the client has paid their last bill she removes the card from its place in the file and puts it at the back of the card box.

Changes to charges   When Mrs Rayner wants to change the charges for livery she has to prepare a letter and a new charge sheet using her word processor. She then sends these to all owners. This usually happens once a year but occasionally if hay or feed gets very expensive she has to put her charges up sooner. She sends the charges out as it saves a lot of people from moaning to her if she hands the charges out personally!

Invoices

At the end of each month, or when an owner is leaving, Sarah and Mrs Rayner get together and work out the bills for each customer. They go through the card index in order to deal with instances where an owner has two horses and so they don't forget where they are up to when the phone rings! The invoices are produced using Word and Sarah prints out a pile ready to use.

To start they need:

- the pile of invoices
- the card file
- Sarah's big diary
- sheets of paper for doing calculations
- a calculator
- envelopes and stamps

What they do   Mrs Rayner takes a card from the card file and the first new invoice sheet from the pile that she has printed out from Word, and fills in the customer's name at the top. She also enters the horse name in the detail section in case there is more than one horse (see Figure 3.4). She then looks at the size of the horse on the card and fills in the basic charge for the month.

Sarah then looks through her book and finds what extras the owner has had during that month for that horse. Sarah has usually prepared a list beforehand on a sheet of paper by going through her diary to make this quicker. The extras are written on to the bill. These are for things like exercising the horse when the owner is away.

Then they check to make sure that the owner has not got another horse. If they have then the charges for that horse are added to the bill. If they haven't then the invoice is totalled, the total added on, folded and put in an envelope. The address is copied from the card. The card is then put back in the file and a new card removed.

Each of these steps is then completed for every owner. Sometimes they have a good day and can get it all done at once. More often there are interruptions and other jobs to be done and they end up having to fit in bits here and there or spend an evening doing the work. Sometimes Sarah has to give Mrs Rayner the list of who has had what and Mrs Rayner has to do all of the bills.

Once the bills are finished they are all sent out together. The copies of the invoices are used to record payments and for the accounts.

I am not going to concern myself with the recording of payments or the accounting side of the business as Mr Rayner does this along with the accounts for his own business and it is Mrs Rayner who wants the records and invoices organising.

This last paragraph shows the student starting to 'firm up' the area of the business that they are concerned with. You tend to get a better idea of exactly what you are going to be looking at as you find out more and get further through the analysis. Don't expect to have all of the answers to begin with!

Notice at this stage that the exact details of the data being entered are not included in the descriptions. This is because you need to start with the processes. Also, having collected the sample documents, you can use them to get most of the details of the data needed.

Everything comes together in what is called a Data Dictionary – more on this later.

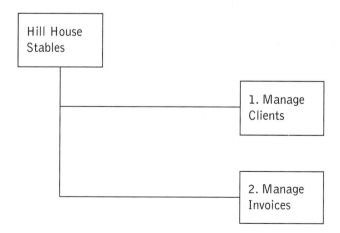

Figure 3.5 Level one decomposition of existing system for Hill House Stables.

Decomposing the system for Hill House Stables

Level one decomposition of existing system

Figure 3.5 shows the two main business processes with which the student is concerned.

Level two decomposition of existing system

In the level two diagram shown in figure 3.6, the two main processes have been broken down into the sub-processes that make them up. You can see that **manage invoices** is made up of just two sub-processes and **manage clients** is made up of six.

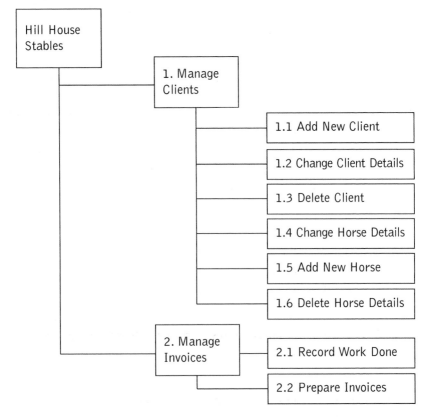

Figure 3.6 Level two decomposition of existing system for Hill House Stables.

Remember that at the moment you are only concerned with the existing system – or what goes on now. If you have chosen a new system to design then you could analyse a similar system and use that to discuss with the user to get your final proposed system.

What names you use are not important but the name should show that something is happening – processing of some sort is taking place.

Level three decomposition of existing system

This is only necessary for the process 2.2. The rest are fairly simple processes – you can see this from the written descriptions, whereas 2.2 has a lot of different steps involved. Figure 3.7 shows process 2.2 broken down into fundamental processes.

Notes

As you work through drawing the decomposition diagrams, you will discover other things that you need to know that you haven't found out yet from the end user. In the example here notice that on the level three diagram (Figure 3.7) the student has included copying and filing the completed invoice – the description doesn't mention these because the student hadn't realised then that they needed to be included.

This is why I recommend that this sort of diagram and dataflow diagrams are drawn to start off with in pencil as you will need to change them several times before they are correct.

Also remember that everyone won't necessarily break down the same system in the same way and certainly would have given different names to the processes. There is no exactness in this work – it is 'best fit' at this level. The markers want to see that you understand the techniques and have tried to use them as well as you can.

You may also be getting an idea of which processes will be left as manual as they are not suited to automation. There may also be too many processes

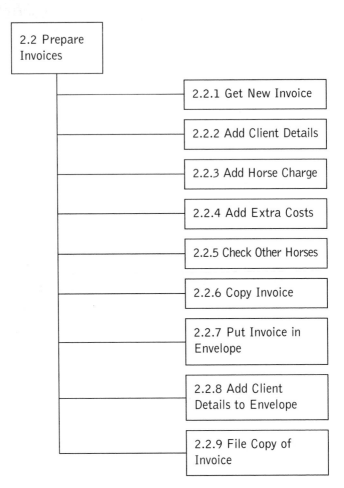

Figure 3.7 Level three decomposition for process 2.2 Prepare Invoices

involved for you to cope with for a project and you may be starting to think which ones to concentrate on. In this example the process of recording the work, process 2.1, stands out as it is necessary for a lot of other reasons besides producing invoices and it is not something that has been highlighted as a problem. Looking at how the stables work it would also be difficult from a practical point of view to automate this.

Notice how by numbering the processes in this way it makes it easy to refer to them – this will be important for the rest of the project. The analysis really is important for lots of reasons so don't give up yet!

Data flow

So what next?

Now you know what goes on in your existing system – what the business or organisation does. You now need to find out what data they need to operate, where the data comes from and what information they produce as a result and who it goes to – generally speaking, the inputs and the outputs.

The easiest way to document this part of the analysis is by using the now, quite old, technique of data flow diagramming.

Some terms you will need to understand

DATA STORE

A place where data is kept. This can be a computer file, a file in a filing cabinet, a card file, an address book, a diary, a pile of letters on a desk, an invoice book and even a waste paper bin! Don't imagine that it has to be a formal file.

PROCESS

An action. Something that causes a change to data or converts data into information. It could be getting a blank invoice, writing on a customer name, looking up a customer address, calculating a total. Any of these are processes; they all include a verb (or doing word). All processes must have something coming into and out of them.

Remember that for information systems it is the processes involving data that concern you.

DATAFLOW

Used to show the movement of data into, between and out of processes and from sources and sinks.

Remember you are not concerned with physical objects moving around e.g. actual products, but the data that goes with them. These include delivery notes, bills, orders, application forms, personnel records, training records, appointment cards and also data transferred electronically or by word of mouth.

SOURCE

Data comes from these into the system. For example a customer is often a source of orders. A supplier will be a source of delivery notes and invoices. Government departments will be the source of data on tax and national insurance rates. The personnel department may be the source of data on employees that is then fed into a training system.

SINK OR DESTINATION

Receives output from the system. This could be the management team at a golf club, government departments collecting VAT returns or PAYE details, the customer receiving an invoice or an employee getting a report.

ENTITY

Something that data is stored about. A customer, supplier, product, invoice, employee and so on. The data stored about them are the attributes of the entity, e.g. name, address, phone number, invoice number, product code etc.

RELATIONSHIP

What links entities together and can be of three types. One to one, one to many or many to many. Check through your theory work on this.

Data flow diagrams

The advantage of DFDs, as they are commonly known, is that they are meant to provide a visual picture of a system that can be used with the end user to ensure that the analyst knows precisely what is happening.

All sets of DFDs should have a key to go with them. There are different symbologies used — it used to be circles for processes but now squares are often used. It really doesn't matter at all what symbols you choose to use so long as you include a key — this is simply good practice with any diagram used in a report. You have got to remember that other people have to be able to understand what you have done and that doesn't just mean your end user and teacher — several markers and moderators could study your project. All of them have got to be able to understand your work. You need to prove what you have done and the easier your project report is to read and find your way around, the better for you.

Symbols used

On all of the data flow diagrams used in this book the symbols are:

Source or destination

Data store

Process

Data flow $\longrightarrow$

System boundary - - - - - - - - -

Note

As I've said it is important that you include a key to the symbols that you use. It doesn't matter what you choose as long as you include a key. Different books use different symbols. I use the ones shown because I find them quicker to draw freehand and data flow diagrams are much easier to do freehand than to produce on a computer. If you do try to do them that way you end up spending far more time fiddling around drawing the diagrams than you do thinking about the content. You can always produce a neat version if you have time or even ink over one drawn in pencil.

Also do make sure that you put titles on all of your diagrams so someone else can follow them through e.g. 'Existing system DFD level 1' or 'Existing system level 2 process 3.1 and 3.2'.

The context diagram

As the name suggests this diagram puts the system that you are looking at into its context – its place in the overall business or outside world. It is important to help you establish the boundaries of the system so that you can identify what are internal and external data sources, entities and data stores.

This is a pretty important diagram as it may show up constraints that you have to work within. An example would be if you are using a customer file that already exists elsewhere within the company then you will have to consider its structure and contents in your system rather than designing one from scratch. It also shows you, or makes you find out, where data comes from into the system or information goes out to – this is where the sample documents that you collected when you did your investigation and observation become useful.

Figure 4.1 shows a level 0 context diagram for the existing system at Hill House Stables which was looked at in the last chapter.

As you can see from the diagram the clients and the staff provide the inputs to the system. These are the personal and horse details and the work done.

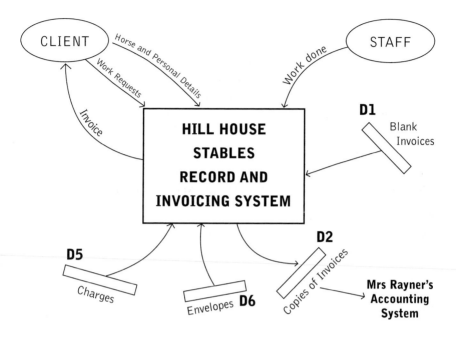

Figure 4.1 Level 0 context diagram for the existing system at Hill House Stables.

Note, you will notice in the higher level diagrams shown in Chapter 3 that the personal and horse details input is broken down in more detail as it is different in different circumstances, but at this stage this is sufficient.

The outputs are the invoice in an envelope sent to the client and the copy of the invoice which goes into the 'copies of invoices' file and eventually into the accounting system.

The data stores D1, D2, D5 and D6 also provide inputs to the system. They are shown on this diagram, as they are what are called **external** files. They exist outside the system and are used in other systems.

For example the blank invoices are produced by Sarah when she is using Word and doing other tasks as well.

If you have external data stores in your system you will have to make sure that you know the exact format that data is stored in in these files.

The level one diagram

From level one downwards the processes have already been identified in the decomposition diagrams shown in Chapter 3 so now you can start asking yourself, or your end user, what is the data needed for process 1 and where does it come from? What is the output from process 1 and where does it go? This logical step-by-step approach actually makes this work easier. In my experience the decomposition helps, as all you are looking at then is processes, you don't have to bother with inputs and outputs. Now because you already know what the processes are there is less to think about. I usually have found that students get bogged down if they just use data flow diagrams because there are so many things to think about at once.

The level one diagram (see figure 4.2) is the hardest to do as it contains all of the high level processes, all of the data stores and data flows.

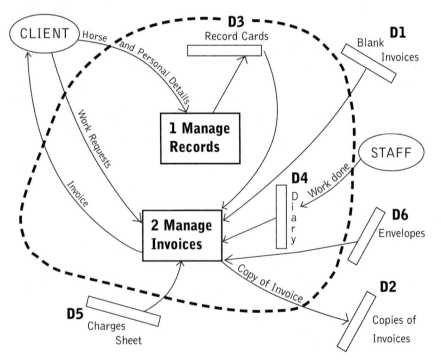

Figure 4.2 Level 1 diagram for the existing system at Hill House Stables.

In the context diagram the system being looked at is shown simply as a box. In this diagram you will notice that the system boundary is clearly shown by a dotted line. Everything that was outside the box in the level 0 diagram is outside this line now. Exactly the same sources, data stores and flows as were on the first diagram are included but with the detail inside of the box added in.

We can now identify data stores D3 and D4 as internal stores – used only within this system, and the two processes from the level one decomposistion diagram. This is why the decomposition helps as once you know the processes it becomes much easier to work out the data flows and the data stores involved.

Level two and three diagrams

How many other diagrams you will need depends on how complex your system is and how far you need to break it down. In the Hill House system there are three more needed – the same as for the decomposition. They are all shown in figures 4.3, 4.4 and 4.5. Notice how on the level two process 1 diagram (see figure 4.3) the data flows are more detailed. Also notice the system boundary is shown on every diagram as a dotted line.

On the level three diagram for process 2.2 (see figure 4.5) there is a distinct shortage of space and the data flows have simply been labelled with letters. The detail of this is found in the next chapter on data flows in the data dictionary.

You should also notice that there are a different number of processes shown in figure 4.5 than there were on the decomposition diagram (figure 3.7). The student has realised that they needed extra ones as they worked through this level. There is nothing wrong with doing this – it all shows you breaking a complex problem down.

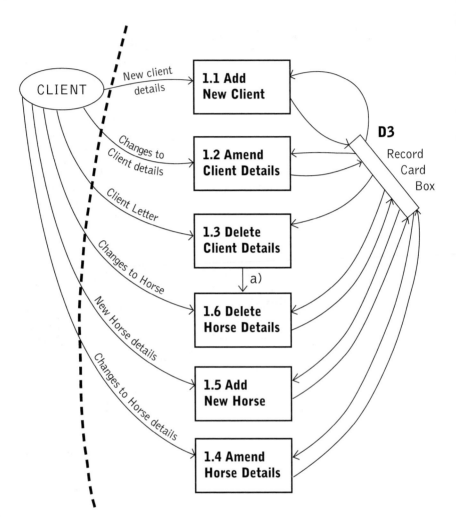

Figure 4.3 Level 2 diagram for process 1 in the existing system at Hill House Stables.

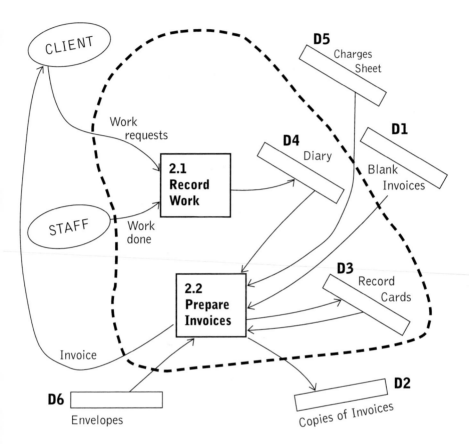

Figure 4.4 Level 2 diagram for process 2 in the existing system at Hill House Stables.

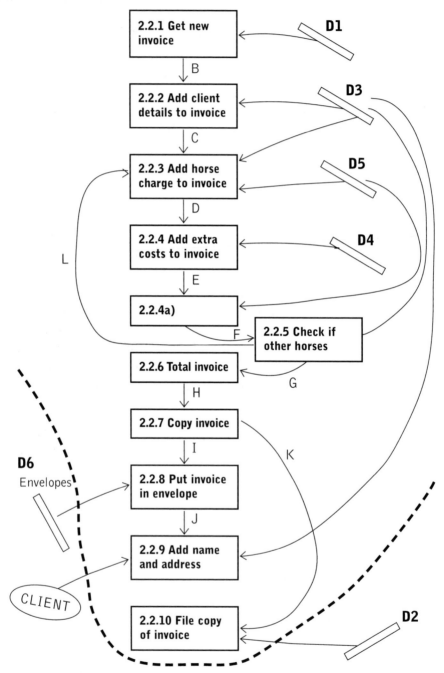

Figure 4.5 Level 3 diagram for process 2.2 in the existing system at Hill House Stables.

Data dictionaries

These are one of the most important elements in any project. They are often poorly done by students who seem to think that the only thing that has to go in is a description of the data stores. This is definitely not the case and it is the descriptions of processes and data flows that actually make the data dictionary so important. In a large organisation where complex systems are being developed there are lots of different people working on projects who all need to be 'speaking the same language', referring to processes by the same name and being able to incorporate the same data stores into each of several different programs being produced by different people. The only way in which this can happen is to have the data dictionary as the definitive reference point which everyone works with.

A data dictionary should also not just include definitions of data. It should include descriptions of all processes, stores, flows, sources and destinations of data and information. In other words it should provide a full description of the system – both existing and proposed.

The next section includes the data dictionary entries for the Hill House Stables example used in previous chapters.

Data dictionary for Hill House Stables' records and invoicing system

Sources and sinks (see definitions)

In this system these are:

Name	Description
Client	Someone who keeps a horse(s) at Hill House Stables.
Staff	Including Sarah, people who work at the stables looking after the horses.

The processes that are shown on the diagrams in the previous chapters need to be described in the data dictionary. The following table shows all of the processes. The descriptions go with the lowest level the process is broken down into. So for process 1 the description of managing horse and client records is made up of the descriptions for processes 1.1 up to process 1.6.

When you write process descriptions the chances are you'll end up changing the data flow diagrams as you suddenly think 'Oh I forgot about having to do that!' In fact this work shows the detailed problem solving and attention to detail that is needed by someone working within ICT. It isn't difficult, it just requires concentration and time, and as mentioned earlier, it isn't the easiest thing to do so don't give up. It means you probably need to go and ask your end user other questions.

	Processes		
Level one	**Level two**	**Level three**	**Description**
1. Manage clients and horse records			
	1.1 Add new client		When a new client joins a blank record card is taken from the card box and the details are written on the front of the card.
	1.2 Amend client details		When a client changes their phone number or moves house etc. then the correct card is found in the card box and the details altered. The card then goes back in the box in the correct position.
	1.3 Delete client details		When a client leaves the correct card is found and put at the back of the box.
	1.4 Add new horse		After the client details have been added the horse details are added to the back of the index card. The card is then filed in the box in alphabetical order of surname.

| | Processes | | |
Level one	Level two	Level three	Description
	1.5 Amend horse details		This happens either when a client replaces one horse with another, or when the feed or problems need to be updated. The correct card is found in the card box and then the horse details are amended. Sometimes one client has several cards – one for each horse. The card is then returned to the box.
	1.6 Delete horse details		When a client sells a horse and doesn't replace it – i.e. when they have more than one horse. The correct card is found in the card box and the horse details are crossed out for the one that is leaving and the card replaced in the card box. If the client leaves this happens as part of process 1.3.

	Processes		
Level one	**Level two**	**Level three**	**Description**
2. Manage invoices			
	2.1. Record work done		Sarah and the other staff record what work they have done in the diary. Clients write in there as well to say things like 'please get my horse in today' or 'exercise Billy on Thursday please'.
	2.2. Prepare Invoices		
		2.2.1 Get new invoice	Take a blank invoice from the pile produced earlier. Also add month and date of invoice.
		2.2.2 Add client details to invoice	Get record card and copy details of client on to invoice.
		2.2.3 Add horse charge to invoice	Look at height of horse on record card, get correct rate from copy of charges and enter on invoice.
		2.2.4 Add extra costs to invoice	Look in diary for previous month and record each extra client has had. This may involve rough work adding up number of exercise sessions.
		2.2.4a)	Look up extra costs on charges sheet and calculate total cost of

	Processes		
Level one	**Level two**	**Level three**	**Description**
			each extra item and add to invoice.
		2.2.5 Check if other horses	Check if there is more than one horse owned and if so repeat 2.2.3. to 2.2.4a for each other horse.
		2.2.6 Total invoice	Add up each extra item total to give invoice total and enter on invoice. A calculator is used for this.
		2.2.7 Copy invoice	Photocopy the invoice to give one copy.
		2.2.8 Put invoice in envelope	Put original invoice in envelope, folded twice. Invoices are A4, envelopes are standard size.
		2.2.9 Add name and address	Copy name and address from card on to envelope and put envelope in pile to post.
		2.2.10 File copy of invoice	Take copy of invoice and put in filing cabinet under 'invoices unpaid'.

Notice process 2.2.4a) – this was a process that originally got missed out and had to be added later when it was discovered it was needed! This sort of thing is quite likely to happen, so don't get worried if it does.

Detailed description of processes

The descriptions of processes used in the table are fairly simple ones. If you want to spend more time on this as you feel it may help later then you can use the format used in the following example to describe each process.

Process 3.4 Produce weekly sales report

Carried out every Monday for the previous Monday to Saturday, inclusive, (current week) sales.

Produced by sales department secretary.

Inputs:

Weekly sales report blank form – from file of two part standard forms (stationery reference E22)

Current weeks sales data – provided by store manager each day on form S4 and filed in date order in daily sales files

Date – date produced from calendar

Week number – current week, calculated from start of financial year (week x)

Outputs

Two copies of weekly sales report for week x – one for sales manager and one for head office

Steps involved

1 Get blank form E22.
2 Get sales data sheets S4 for previous week.
3 Enter date.
4 Enter week number.
5 Enter each day's sales on to E22 by day and by category – see data store D3 for details of form layout.
6 Add sales for each department for each day to produce department sub-totals and fill in on form.
7 Add sales by day to produce daily sub-totals and fill in.

8 Add daily sales totals together to get total for week and fill in.

9 Sign form.

10 Split form into two separate parts.

11 Send one copy to head office.

12 Put other copy in sales manager's in-tray with daily sales sheets attached.

You can see from this that the detail of the inputs needed and the outputs produced is given. There is information about who carries out the process when and where. This could be needed so that the analyst can go back to the person actually performing the task to check whether designs for a new system would suit them or if there are more questions that they need to ask.

In the example you may think that the student could have broken this process down into more sub-processes – for example by splitting 5, 6, 7, and 8 off. This is to show you that it isn't a disaster if you don't do this when you are doing your own process analysis.

The aim of project work is not for you to produce the most wonderful commercial standard piece of work. It is for you to show that you understand what is involved and have tried out formal methods in a real environment and discovered the advantages and problems for yourself. If you think about it you will realise that to check everything is precisely correct the marker would have to undertake the same level of analysis as you!

In the next section you will see how to describe the actual data flows, inputs and outputs in the system in the data dictionary.

Data analysis

Data analysis is about finding out exactly what data is needed within the system.

The first stage is to look at the data flows that you have included on your diagrams and to write these up in the data dictionary.

The data flows in the system show the movement of data between processes. Movements back and to data stores are not generally labelled. If, like me, you have a job thinking of names for them or don't have enough space to write a name on the flow, then just give them simple labels and give a full description in the data dictionary – this is much easier.

The descriptions try to make clear all of the 'bits' of data that are moving through the system. Also included here are the inputs to, and outputs from, the system. These are the labelled flows that cross the system boundary line and go to a source or sink.

Curly brackets { } represent a repeating group of items, something that can appear zero or more times in the data flow.

Notice that in the examples used in the previous chapters and in the following table, a lot of the data flows can be identified by pieces of paper. The hardest ones are the ones where data is passed verbally, in a person's mind, or in an existing computerised system.

Data flow label/name	Description
A	Record cards for client who is leaving i.e. horse details
B	Blank invoice
C	Blank invoice + client name + {horse name}
D	Blank invoice + client name + horse charge
E	Blank invoice + client name + horse charge + {extra description + number + unit price + total}
F	Blank invoice + client name + horse charge + {extra description + number + unit price + {extra total}}
G	Blank invoice + client name + {horse charge + {extra description + number + unit price + {extra total}}}
H	Blank invoice + client name + {horse charge + {extra description + number + unit price + {extra total}}} + invoice total
I	Original completed invoice + client name + {horse charge + {extra description + number + unit price + {extra total}}} + invoice total
J Invoice	Envelope + original completed invoice + client name + {horse charge + {extra description + number + unit price + {extra total}}} + invoice total
K Copy of invoice	Copied completed invoice + client name + {horse charge + {extra description + number + unit price + {extra total}}} + invoice total
L	Blank invoice + client name + {horse charge + {extra description + number + unit price + {extra total}}}

Horse and personal details	Input from client broken up into the following flows on level 2 process 1 DFD
New client details	Client name + address + {phone numbers} + blacksmith + vet + {child name} + {{horse name} + age + sex + height + feed + problems}
Change to details	Client name + {change to item e.g. phone number}
Client letter	Client name + contains leaving date of client
Changes to horse	Client name + leaving date of horse + {leaving date of client}
New horse details	Client name + {{horse name} + age + sex + height + feed + problems}
Changes to horse details	Client name + {changes to horse details}
Work requests	Client name + horse name + work (extra) needed
Work done	Horse name + work done

At the moment you don't have the details of exactly what is in each data store: what a customer name is; the possible heights of horses and so on. To find out exactly what the data is like you now need to go back to the sample documents that you have collected and analyse them in detail.

Document analysis sheet

The document analysis sheet is something that you can make up for yourself or a teacher may provide you with. The idea of it is to make you study sample documents and look at the type of data they contain.

DOCUMENT NUMBER	DOCUMENT NAME	OTHER NAMES OR REFERENCES
SIZE	NUMBER OF PARTS	MEDIUM
PREPARED BY?	HOW OFTEN PREPARED?	HOW MANY?
FILED WHERE?	IN WHAT ORDER?	HOW LONG KEPT?
WHO GETS IT?	FOR WHAT PURPOSE?	GROWTH?

ITEM	TYPE	SIZE	OCCURENCE	VALUE RANGE	SOURCE

Figure 6.1 Document analysis sheet.

NAME/ADDRESS OF PERSON BOOKING or Agent's Stamp

Mr/~~Mrs/Miss~~	R J WILSON
Address	44 WOLFORD CRESC
	WOODSTOCK
	WESTSHIRE Postcode WE3 5QY
Telephone Day 0793 846592 Evening 01724 333111	

Agent's ref ....RJW/AB/02.......   ER ref ....ER/1124...........

TRAVEL DETAILS

Number of nights __7__   Departure date __21/07/02__

Departure Airport __MANCHESTER__

UK connecting flight from

Airport _____   Date _____

Seating preference (if possible) __AISLE__

NAMES OF ALL PERSONS TRAVELLING

Mr Mrs Miss	Forename	Surname	**IMPORTANT** Please specify type of passport (ie, British, US, Australian, etc.)	Date of birth (if under 12)	BA Executive Card no.
MR	RICHARD	WILSON	BRITISH	/	/
MRS	JENNIFER	WILSON	''	/	/

DESTINATION DETAILS

Destination	Hotel/Cruise/Yacht	Type of Accommodation (if applicable)	No. of nights	No. of rooms	No meals	Bed/ B'fast	Half Board	Full Board
CYPRUS	HOTEL BONIFACIO	/	7	1			/	

Figure 6.2 Booking form.

DOCUMENT NUMBER	DOCUMENT NAME	OTHER NAMES OR REFERENCES
①	Booking form page one .	—

SIZE A4 Landscape	NUMBER OF PARTS 2	MEDIUM Paper (2 part pad)
PREPARED BY? Booking clerk	HOW OFTEN PREPARED? Once per client	HOW MANY? 10 – 15 each day
FILED WHERE? Bookings file	IN WHAT ORDER? ER Reference	HOW LONG KEPT? 12 months.
WHO GETS IT? Customer one copy One kept filed	FOR WHAT PURPOSE? – Confirms booking	GROWTH? None expected .

ITEM	TYPE	SIZE	OCCURENCE	VALUE RANGE	SOURCE
Agents Ref	Text	8	1	Any value like XXX/XX/99.	From Travel Company
ER Ref	"	7	1	Any value like XX/9999	Reason. Already Produced on sheet
Name	"	?30	1	Any Initials+ Surname	Client
Title	"	3	1	MR, MRS, MISS	" .
Address/	"	?30	1	Any	"
2	"	?30	1		"
3	"	?30	1	↓ .	"
Postcode .	"	8	1	XX99 99XX	"
Telephone Day Number	12	1		"
Evening	"	12	1		"
No o/nights	"	2	1	3,4,7,14,21	Client .
Dept Date	Date	8	1	*Must be over current date +30	"
Airport	Text	20	1	(List of Uk airports)	Client
Date	Date	8	1	as *	Client
Seating Pref.	Text	10	1	Aisle or Window	" .
Title Name	Text	3	1 or more	MR, MRS, MISS.	"
Forename	Text	30	1 or more		"
Surname	Text	30	"		"
Passport .	Text	20	"	From list	– Checked against national passport list.
DoB.	Date	8	"		"
BA Card No	Num	7	"	U/T O 9999999	" .

Figure 6.3 Document analysis sheet for the booking form.

A brief description of each of the fields on the analysis form is as follows:

- Document number – given by you to each document
- Document name – what you are calling it
- Other names – sometimes a form is called one thing by one person and something else by someone else e.g. some people could say 'form 82' or others 'customer booking form'
- Size – e.g. A4 or A5
- Number of parts – is it multi part stationery used?
- Medium – paper, carbonised paper, printout etc.
- Prepared by – who fills it in
- How often – some idea of how often it is done
- How many – an idea of the volumes involved
- Filed – where is it stored?
- In what order – very important as this indicates possible key fields
- How long kept – helps to explain when system needs updating and archiving
- Who gets it and for what purpose – helps in design, also from data flow diagrams
- Growth – have you got to allow for more or less in the new system

Figure 6.1 shows a sample document analysis sheet. Figure 6.2 shows part of a booking form used in a travel company. Figure 6.3 shows a document analysis form that a student has started to fill in for the booking form. Notice that this is not complete and the student would need to continue on to a second sheet. You will find that these are again not difficult to do – it just takes time, patience and attention to detail. It is amazing how the simplest form actually has an awful lot of different items of data on it. There is no right or wrong way to complete something like this when you are using it in project work. Its purpose is to help you and so long as it does then it has been useful.

As well as looking at sample documents you can look at records in computerised and manual files (your data stores) in the same way to discover the detail of the data needed and used by the system.

What the forms can do is to provide you with a list of data items within the system as your starting point for normalisation for a database.

Other techniques that can be used in analysis

It is impossible to cover every technique that you could use to analyse and document a system. You may find that your teacher shows you other techniques such as four sector diagrams or decision tables. It really does not matter what you use so long as the end result is a well documented analysis that shows you all of the elements that make up the existing system.

The next step

Having completed your decomposition and/or data flow diagrams or used some other technique to analyse the existing system, the next stage is to find out some more from your end user. At the moment you don't know what they think is wrong with the existing system or whether there are other things that they want a new system to do. So the question now is 'what else do I need to know about?'

Here is a checklist of the things that you should go and find out about. Some of these will have already been mentioned when you were working on your AS projects. Exactly which of these are most important and whether, for example, security is an issue or not will depend on your individual project.

- Resources available
  - hardware
  - software
  - human skill level
- Constraints/limitations
  - maybe resources available
  - special requirements
  - security
  - logistics
  - data protection
- Problems with the current system
  - what doesn't it do that is wanted?
  - what is wrong with what it does do?

When you have done this your next job is to get your end user's requirements – which is just what you had to do for your AS project. I always think of it as an equation:

$$\frac{\text{Existing}}{\text{system}} + \frac{\text{User}}{\text{requirements}} + \frac{\text{Constraints/}}{\text{limitations}} \rightarrow \text{Proposed solution}$$

Once you have the user's requirements you can set the performance criteria for the proposed system (see Chapter 6 in the AS book).

| The proposed system

Having modelled the existing system and having found out the user's requirements for and constraints upon any solution that you develop, you now need to show the model of your proposed system.

So do you need to do more diagrams and a data dictionary? The answer is yes, but there are easy ways to do this.

First of all start by photocopying what you have done for the existing system and then add on or remove any unwanted processes or extra ones needed. In the same way leave what you already have in the data dictionary and add a section at the end to show new processes, flows or data stores that are needed. Generally, the changes that you will find that you need to make are things like:

- adding on processes to produce reports – the most frequent requirement
- adding on processes to improve security of data or validity of data
- making processes automatic that are currently manual e.g making multiple copies of documents
- removing processes that are going to remain manual to outside the system boundary
- combining existing data stores –where two or more stores have data on the same entity

- making data stores external where you discover someone else needs to use them as well – a common example here is where stock files are used by a shop branch and the central company office
- having extra data stores that you hadn't realised were needed before

In the Hill House Stables example, the diary was turned into an external data store and excluded from the system, as it was actually used by the staff working at the stables for deciding on the day's work and allocating jobs, ordering feed and blacksmiths' visits. Also the process of recording work done was not really part of the record keeping and invoice production, and so was excluded. The data provided by it was in the diary and so this was an input to the proposed system.

The task of putting invoices into envelopes was also moved out of the proposed system to remain a manual task.

The production of blank invoices was combined into the process of producing an invoice as this could be done using the software that was chosen to implement the new system, and didn't need to be outside it.

Mrs Rayner decided that it would be really useful to have a list of unpaid invoice totals with names each month so that she knew when someone had paid and could stop having to remind them or ask them if they had. This was a new process.

Look at your own existing systems and see if there are examples of things like these that you can exclude or add.

It is at this point that you and your teacher may think that you need to 'suggest' to your end user that some reporting processes or other functions might be a good idea. This does not stop your project being realistic but helps when your end user doesn't have any idea as to what extra information the proposed system could give him.

For example, Mrs Rayner could have a process to calculate the feed needed for the horses each day and produce a weekly order list for the suppliers. She is not likely to know that this is possible – a clear example of how ICT can help a business by producing information that would otherwise be too costly or time consuming to produce. In this case Mrs Rayner

would have to go through all of the horse record cards manually to extract the feed information and then categorise and sum it.

At the end of the analysis phase you should have:

- Existing system
  - processes
  - boundary
  - data stores
  - dataflows
  - inputs and outputs
  - constraints/limitations
    human
    software
    hardware
    financial
- Proposed system
  - end user requirements
  - performance criteria
  - processes
  - boundary
  - data stores
  - dataflows
  - inputs and outputs

The only other thing that you will need will be an idea of your time planning for the other stages of the project.

Note

If you don't analyse your system properly you will have several problems:

- you will have difficulty with designing a solution,
- you will have problems in implementing the solution,
- you will find it difficult to test a solution when you don't know what it is supposed to do,

- you will find it difficult to evaluate your solution as you won't know what your criteria should be,
- you will find documenting the report much more difficult as you won't have a logical structure to it, and
- you won't get many marks for the analysis section!

Remember what the criteria are that you are trying to meet in order to gain high marks on the analysis. Look also at the mark allocations for each section of the project and see how much weighting the analysis section has – then you will realise why it has taken you so long to do it!

Design for A2 projects

Much of what you need to include in design work has already been covered in your AS work. This section aims to look at the extra things that you must do for A2.

Considering alternative solutions and selecting the most suitable

Many students lose marks on this because the extent of their ideas for alternative solutions is to consider implementing their proposed solution using different generic software packages. This is not really appropriate in most cases as each piece of generic software is better suited to some tasks than others and it is probably quite obvious that the problem that you have is most suited to one particular one. This means that if you have what is obviously a proposal that needs solving using database management software, you will be giving very weak ideas as to why it could be implemented using a word-processing program!

So what can you do instead? Consider the following:

- Would some of the system be better manual or automated?
- Where should the system boundary go?
- Is there justification for automating at all?
- What are the advantages of your proposed solution over a manual system?
- Is the best solution one using a combination of software packages or

a single package? For example do you export data to a word processing package to print reports or do it within the software that you
are using? Would you combine the use of spreadsheet software and
relational database management software to use the best features of
both?

- Could you use different features within the same software or a different design within the same software?
- Should the company buy an 'off-the-shelf package' or a bespoke
solution?

What does the marker want to know?

They want to know that now you have your end user's requirements and
the performance criteria you can make logical well-argued decisions on the
best method of solution. Sometimes this is not easy when you will have
been told that 'You will use a relational database management software
package to implement your major project'!

What about differences in menu design and structure? Could you consider alternatives like that?

Here is an example:

In a vets' surgery the vets and the receptionists use the appointment system. They use
the system in different ways and their requirements of, and familiarity with, the system are quite different. The vets use the system infrequently to look at future book-
ings, to generate reports on common reasons for visits, frequency of client visits and
so on and to conduct one-off research.

The receptionists use the system every day to make appointments and to add, amend
and delete pet and owner details as well as to give the vets their daily appointment
schedules. One proposed menu structure is shown in Figure 8.1

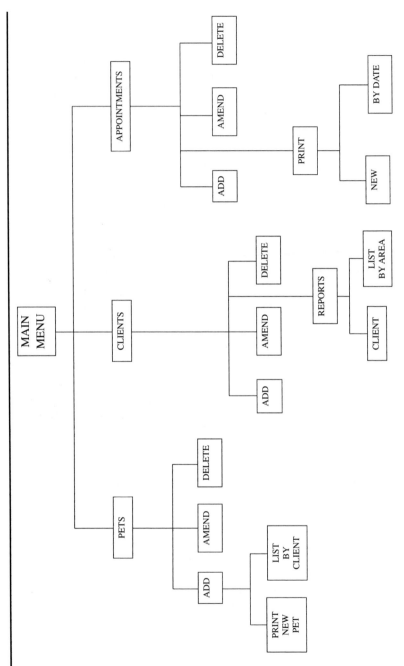

Figure 8.1 One possible structure for the vets' system.

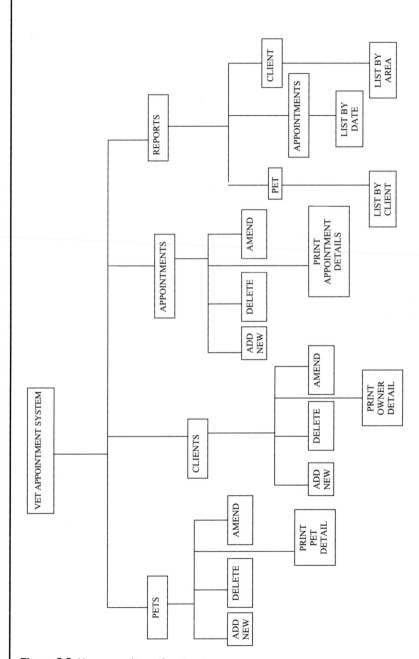

Figure 8.2 Shows an alternative structure.

In the first design the vets would have to keep moving down through the menu hierarchy to get to the features that they want to use. Even if they had shortcuts provided they are unlikely to remember these as they are infrequent users. The result of this is that they would not consider the system easy to use and would probably gain little from it. Putting security on to the functions that the vets use would be more difficult with this structure. If the vets wanted additional reporting features, the structure could become difficult to work with and major changes could be needed.

In the second option (see figure 8.2) all of the problems above have been addressed without making the system any harder for the receptionists to use. It would allow changes to be made if the vets require additional management information without major changes to the rest of the solution – this means easier enhancements.

So as you can see from the diagrams, one solution is much more suitable than the other and any evaluation of these alternatives against the user requirements would show this.

My message is really think about **practical** options and don't just assume your alternatives have to be totally different pieces of software.

How to assess the alternatives

When choosing a solution to a problem the best way to do it is to be objective. This avoids a lot of unnecessary waffle or scoring systems (although these can be useful in some situations). You have a set of user requirements and a set of performance criteria so why not use those as the measures of which solution is best?

Also as part of your theory work you will have covered evaluation criteria so why not use these as well? This way you end up with a much more balanced and logical decision that will help to gain you more marks.

Assessment criteria for marking the project state that

> 'A *relevant* range of approaches to a solution has been considered in *detail.* *Compelling* reasons for final choice of solution have been given which have been *justified* and the *likely effectiveness* has been *fully* considered.'

The italicised words are the ones that you need to concentrate on if you are to get good marks on this part of the design.

So a good consideration of solutions will take several alternatives in turn and consider how well each meet the performance criteria and end user requirements before concluding with 'compelling reasons' for the final choice.

Entities and relationships

Many A2 projects are based on database solutions. If these are used then it is essential that you look at the entities and relationships within your system.

A marker will look at your entity relationship diagram and your normalised data to see whether you have a relational database or not and how efficient it is.

It is not within the scope of this book to discuss how to normalise your data or the theory of entities and relationships as these are covered in many other books, but here are some hints for making sure your structures are correct:

1   As you analyse your existing system try to identify the entities involved and draw a rough diagram up. Do not worry about the type of relationships between them at this stage. You may find that you actually have very few entities at this stage.
2   Use the information that you gain from the data analysis to provide the starting point for normalisation. If you do this properly you will already have picked up where you have data that is calculated or occurs multiple times.
3   When you have completed your proposed design and normalised your data revise your entity relationship diagram. This is when you will discover that you have a lot more entities than you first thought!

4   You should not have many-to-many relationships as this results in repetition of data and inefficiency in your solution. It also means that the database you think you have will be impossible to build.

5   Normalisation gives you your entities and the entity relationship diagram shows the relationships between them.

6   Don't forget to describe the relationships between entities. For example in the Hill House Stables exercise, two entities are clients and horses. One client can own many horses but one horse is only owned by one client – so this is a one-to-many relationship, client to horse.

7   If you have one-to-one relationships you shouldn't! Or there must be a very good reason for doing it.

8   No data store should contain calculated fields – this would give you redundant data.

9   Watch what happens if data is deleted from one data store that is linked to another. In the Hill House case should you be able to delete client's details without deleting their horse's details? If you delete a record that is associated with another without deleting that you end up with 'floating data' not related to anything else and totally useless.

10 Think carefully about your key fields – these should emerge from normalisation. You must think about the information that you need to get out of the system and whether your data stores are linked in a way that makes this possible. I have seen an awful lot of students who couldn't generate reports that the end user wanted because they hadn't sorted out relationships and key fields properly!

11 Think practically – all of the rules and the whole background to relational databases is logical and common sense so think of it that way – not as a difficult bit of theory.

Note

A primary key is one that uniquely identifies an occurrence of an entity. For example your candidate number uniquely identifies you to the examination board.

A foreign key is where the primary key for one entity is used as a foreign key for another entity so that the fields can be used to link the entities together when needed. An example here would be a product that has a product code that uniquely identifies them – the primary key for the product data store. An order is to be prepared showing the product code and a description of the product that has been ordered. The entity order will contain the foreign key product code so that when the order is produced the product description can be obtained as needed from the product data store, without having to be stored as part of the order data store as well as the product data store.

Be careful that if you **should** have a relational database structure to your solution, you **do** have. There is no 'norm' to the number of entities involved. If your structure is looking too 'simple' at this point, then discuss it with your teacher. Reassess what else you could include in the system that the end user could find useful and suggest it to them. An example here would be if you were simply keeping details of members of a leisure club and their subscription payments. This would be a one-to-one relationship between member and payment. You could suggest incorporating something like keeping details of which club facilities they used or teams they belonged to. Generally if you have chosen a suitable system for the project this shouldn't give you much of a problem – if in doubt discuss this early on with your teacher.

Other considerations in design

One of the important aspects of your analysis that will help in the rest of your project is the breaking down of a complex task into sub-tasks and **numbering** them **systematically**. Now you can use this numbering to refer to each process and you can design each numbered process in turn so that your design is for solutions to processes.

Many projects have designs for the elements of the solution, e.g. tables, reports, forms and queries, etc. Although this can be one way of approaching the design work, it is more effective to do it by process, as then you are concentrating on what the solution should do. This in turn makes implementation and testing easier.

I always say that I want to be able to see a process identified in the analysis then designed, implemented and tested. The numbering helps to give a consistency and structure to the work and helps you to know where you are up to!

Having designed a solution to a task for your AS project, you should find that you will be able to use the knowledge and skills for your A2 project. Additionally you will have to consider what else a marker will want to see. Consider the following points for each of the three criteria given below:

> 'A *completely detailed* solution has been specified so that it could be undertaken by a *competent third party*. The proposed solution has been *clearly* broken down into sub-tasks, with the necessary indications of how those are to be solved. *All* requirements are specified and *clearly* documented.'

- If you have analysed your system carefully then you should be able to show the design for the overall system and how the components will fit together. Don't forget to consider how the system will be implemented on the end user's hardware and software. Will you need to create folders or shortcuts for them? Where will archived data be saved? You should know the detail needed in designs for third party implementation from AS.
- Remember this is a cyclical solution so there needs to be a design for archiving and 'cleaning' down the system for the next time period or event. For example at the end of the financial year what happens to paid and unpaid invoice details? After a sports event what data is saved for the next event and what is removed? As students move up to the next year in a school how is this to be catered for?
- Documentation to a high standard is crucial – without it the marks cannot be awarded, even if you have thought things through.

> 'A *well-defined* schedule and work plan have been included, showing *in detail* how the task is to be undertaken. This explains what is required in a *comprehensible manner* – it can include layout sheets, record structures, spreadsheet plans, design for data capture sheets, as appropriate.'

- Your data dictionary will enable you to work through each of the processes and data stores, inputs and outputs, in the data dictionary to show the designs for sub-tasks.
- You need to consider the order in which you will implement each of the sub-tasks and how they will be linked together. For example you cannot build queries to extract data if you haven't already built the data stores, added data to them and tested these elements first.
- Plans should not just be token Gantt charts that show very little. They need to be what you actually plan to do. Now you are dealing with a system rather than an individual task the management of the work is far more crucial – this is why project management tools are used in industry. The bigger and more complex the system the more important planning is. You can't achieve an A2 project in a weekend!

'An *effective* and *full* testing plan has been devised, with a comprehensive selection of test data and reasons for the choice of data clearly specified.'

- The testing plan must be comprehensive but not full of lots of repetitive validation tests or 'button pushing' tests.
- The test plan must include testing of the system as a whole and the cyclical features.
- The test plan must include end user testing by your real end user.
- You must justify the data that you are using to test. Where will you get this from? Can your end user provide you with the data? Sample documents are the best sources of real data, but be careful about not disclosing real names and addresses.
- Consider how much data you are going to need to fully test queries and reports. You can't fully test a multi-page report when you only have five records in your data source!
- How will you test the cyclical features?
- Effective means that you have made sure that your system does what it is supposed to do – that it works, it does what the end user wants. It needs to meet their requirements and your performance criteria. So don't forget to have the requirements and criteria there when you are designing the plan!

9

Implementation, testing and user guide

Implementation

> 'The candidate has *fully* implemented the *detailed design unaided*, in an *efficient manner* with no *obvious defects*. All the *appropriate facilities* of the software *and* hardware available were *fully* exploited. The documentation is *clear and thorough*.'

Let's look at what each of these italicised points means.

Fully implemented – this means that you have completed what you set out to achieve. The important thing is that you don't take on too big a system in the first place. If when you analyse it you think it is too big then cut down what you are going to do for the project, as it will gain you more marks if you complete it. Discuss problems with your teacher, they will be able to suggest ways of maximising your marks in the time available. For example if you have to add, amend and delete, and produce queries and reports on both customers and suppliers, then do all of one first as then you will show a range of skills. Once you have done the customer the supplier will be straightforward.

If the end user wants it all then try negotiating with them to finish it in the holidays, and perhaps get paid for it! Some of my students have done this in the past.

Detailed design unaided – this doesn't mean that your teacher can't help you at all and that you just have to disappear off for hours and waste time because you are stuck. This is a piece of work throughout which you are expected to learn how to do things. Let's say you are stuck with how to produce a multi-page report with totalling on each page, or a query you have tried isn't working. You can ask for help and the teacher can show you with another example so that you can then go back and apply what you have learnt to your own work.

This is part of the teacher's normal role and as such you don't have to worry about it. If they feel they have had to give you more help than anyone else then it is up to them to say so on the mark sheet that they fill in. If you get help from another source, a relative or friend or a textbook then you must say so. Failure to disclose help could result in penalties for cheating!

It is always worth asking for help as if you don't get it and can't implement your design then you can lose more marks as your system will not be fully implemented.

Efficient manner, **appropriate** facilities and **fully** exploited – this means that you have used the best design that you could and that you used the advanced features of the software package(s) used in the most effective way. Projects where the student has tried to use several pieces of software to produce their system often fail on this criteria as the students don't get to know the software very well and do not produce an efficient solution using advanced features. They end up with what I would describe as 'wide and shallow' projects rather than 'narrow and deep' – which is what you are after at this level.

No **obvious** defects – it does what it is supposed to do with no mistakes that the marker can see. Sometimes systems that appear perfect will fail when they are used to extremes – for example with very high volumes of data. It is usually impossible for the average student to test this type of situation and it is also something that the markers can't spot. It does mean that if you have a multi-page report you must include sufficient data to be able to get multiple pages when you test it. If your system is to deal with appointments, then you must be able to make them, amend them and delete them when the record of them is no longer needed or someone cancels, if this is what the user requires. In other words, just like an AS project, the solution must do what it is supposed to do.

Software **and** hardware – look back on what was said about this earlier, and in the AS book, but do consider the capabilities of a printer when producing reports, appropriate back up and archiving media, the eventual size of the data stores and therefore speed of querying. The methods of data input and devices used are important – for example, more mouse and less keyboard or vice versa; laptop or stand-alone PC or network?

The documentation is **clear and thorough** – if the marker cannot see what you have done from your documentation then you can't get the marks. Remember that the marker does not want to learn how to use the piece of software. They want to see how you have used the software to implement the system that you have produced. Also remember the fact that if you design by process and implement by process it makes it easier to document clearly. Again having all processes labelled and listed in a data dictionary makes it easier to do this. Do remember to make printouts clear for the reader to see without a magnifying glass!

Apart from ensuring that you meet the criteria as described above, the most important thing about the implementation is that you don't spend too long on it at the cost of other sections – remember how the marks are allocated! And don't do it before the analysis and design!

Testing

'The candidate has shown insight in demonstrating *effective* test data to cover *most or all* eventualities. There is *clear* evidence of *full user involvement* in testing. The system works with a *full range* of test data (typical, extreme, erroneous), the test outputs are *fully* annotated.'

Most of these requirements are no different to those for testing an AS project. The differences are that you are now testing a system, so there must be full evidence that the system works, not just individual tasks. For example in a system producing reports on students, data about a student must be taken right through to the final report being generated. If the system produces summary reports on a group of students then this must be shown with a group of data used. If the system has to be 'cleaned out' before the next term or year the evidence that this works must be shown.

Additionally end user testing is seen as being absolutely critical. This should not take the form of a token letter written by a friend but should be designed for when the testing plan is produced. Full involvement of end users can be shown from the analysis stage onwards with items such as the analysis of the existing system, end user requirements and designs being 'signed off'.

End users are often very bad at knowing what you want them to do to test a software solution. If you were asked to test a new pair of training shoes you would have some ideas, but you probably wouldn't think about seeing how they washed, or what happened if you ran 50 kilometres continuously in them. Computer end users are the same unless they themselves are used to producing and testing software solutions **in a logical and rigorous way.**

It is often a good idea to 'suggest' the testing that you want the end user to do. You might give them a pre-prepared sheet of instructions and questions to complete. An example of part of one of these is shown below. If you do do this then you need to go back to the end user's requirements and make sure that the testing that you get them do will prove whether your solution meets their requirements or what the problems/limitations of it are. This will then give you the evidence that you need to include in your evaluation section.

Here are some examples of questions that you could ask your end user. There are some examples for different types of solutions.

- How clear were the instructions for installing the Invoicing solution?
- Did you find the user guide helpful in explaining any error messages that you had?
- Did you find the customer report easy to produce? Did it meet your requirements?
- Has the task of preparing a menu been speeded up?
- Do customers find the leaflet on the hotel attractive? Have you had any comments?

- Did you experience any problems deleting a pet's details from the database?
- Were your audience kept interested by the presentation?
- Did you find it easy to update the web page showing match reports?
- Have you had any emails sent as a result of having the website.

Obviously there are lots more questions that you could ask but don't just give the user the solution and ask how they found it – you are unlikely to get anything useful back from them.

Remember that even if you have done a project where your teacher is the end user, you need to have end user testing included – this is one of the reasons why it is much easier to actually have a real one who is not your teacher.

The key point is that the end user needs to be able to test the system against their requirements. Sometimes it is impossible to do this as the system would need to be running for some time before all functions would be used. Also remember that if you have different end users, for example the vets and receptionists, you need to get both to test the system as their requirements will have been different.

Be careful that you leave sufficient time for the end user to test the system. They tend to be busy people and you can't just expect them to drop everything, just because you have a project deadline! You may need to go out to their office or home and demonstrate the system in operation first and this all takes time.

Don't forget that the user guide should be prepared before the end user tests the system as it is part of it. You may want to leave time to make alterations to this after the end user has tested it.

User Guide

'A comprehensive, *well-illustrated* user guide has been produced that deals with *all* aspects of the system (installation, back up procedures, general use and troubleshooting).'

Here is a list of things that should be considered when preparing the user guide for your solution:

1 The language used must reflect the end user. For small children this must be simple, for inexperienced users it should not contain technical terms. Users do not talk in terms of tables and queries.

2 The use of screenshots should be considered essential so that the user can relate this directly to what they are seeing as they use the system. It is not only difficult to write a guide without illustrating it, but makes it very hard for the user to know if they are looking at the right thing!

3 Attention to detail is important. If the user needs to press return after entering data into a field, then tell them they need to. Similarly, if data needs to be entered in capital letters then examples in the guide should illustrate this. If you have ever tried to search a database that has data stored in capitals only and have entered lower case values you will know how frustrating this can be. If you have used an on-line data entry form which doesn't tell you whether to use tab or return to move between fields you will also understand this!

4 The actual installation of the system needs to be described, the level of detail being dependent on who the specified end user is. Even if you are installing the solution for the end user, they should still know what is needed for it to work effectively if this is an issue.

5 Start up procedures must be included and should be for the intended end user in their intended environment. They should not explain how to start the software on the school/college network system unless this is the end user's environment!

6 The normal working of the system should be covered methodically – the flow of the guide should follow the way the end user will work with the system. Start by describing how to enter data if this will be the first thing that the user has to do, don't start with printing out reports or similar. It may be suitable to just describe normal working and not confuse the reader by including error messages, or you may feel it is better to introduce these where they might occur in the use of the solution.

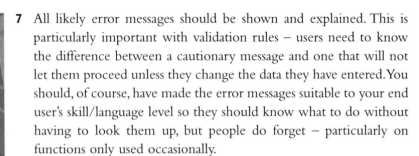

7 All likely error messages should be shown and explained. This is particularly important with validation rules – users need to know the difference between a cautionary message and one that will not let them proceed unless they change the data they have entered. You should, of course, have made the error messages suitable to your end user's skill/language level so they should know what to do without having to look them up, but people do forget – particularly on functions only used occasionally.

8 It should always be made clear to the user what actions they need to take. Never leave an end user not knowing what to do next – this is a basic principle of good design, so make sure the user guide follows it.

9 Saving data/files should be included if this is part of the solution. This should describe what do do in the end user's environment. Watch out for references to saving on p drive on the college/school network!

10 Back up procedures must be approached from a similar angle and should be included in most user guides.

11 Security issues and settings – if these are relevant then they should be included in the guide, including what to do if you forget your password!

12 As the system should be of a 'cyclical' nature, the user guide must include how to archive old data or set up a new financial year or prepare the system for the next sporting tournament.

13 A glossary of terms may be included if this is necessary to the user's understanding of the manual. This is like a dictionary at the end of the guide (or the beginning) that explains any technical terms used. In most cases this will not be necessary if the language used in the guide is appropriate.

14 A quick reference guide may be an appropriate addition for more experienced users. This could take a variety of forms. This could be a simple piece of card that fits in a top pocket or over the function keys, which has reminders of shortcut combinations for macros and other actions. This could also be a more appropriate format where there are many infrequent users of the software who only perform simple tasks.

15 The physical environment that the system is to be operated in may be important to the type of guide produced. For example, space may be tight and a large A4 guide would not be useable in the space available. A small child would need something small and easy to hold that is produced on perhaps stiffer card rather than paper. A user guide used in a kitchen or a factory may need to be coated to prevent it from wearing out too soon in a harsh environment. Also think about how it is to be bound together.

16 The overall structure of the guide is important. Is an index necessary? Should be a list of contents be included? Are page numbers needed?

An increasing number of students like to produce on-line help of various types instead or as well as a user guide. Here are some points to consider if you do.

- Do not spend too much time on it. Look at how many marks you can get and adjust your time accordingly. If it means you won't get the testing done or an evaluation completed, then it is probably better to stick to an ordinary guide.
- Look at good and bad examples of on-line help. Be critical, what annoys you or do you find hard to use? Some common criticisms are:
  - I can't find what I want without knowing what it's called.
  - The help comes up on top of what I want help about so I still don't know what I did wrong.
  - I can't view the help and the work at the same time.
  - It isn't clear what I need to do.
- Are resources an issue – remember sophisticated on-line help is 'resource hungry' and can slow things down.
- Is it actually the best way of doing it? Sometimes the most technically advanced option is not the best. Many people still like to use books. This is perhaps particularly true of older users. Very few of you will have end users who are younger/the same age as yourselves.
- What are you trying to prove? This is the user guide being assessed, not your technical ability.

- Good projects that gain high marks do not need to have on-line help, it is not an essential part of the project.
- If you have done it then it will need testing and you will need to show the contents and how it works very clearly, with clear easy-to-read screenshots.

Above all, make sure that the user guide is suitable for your system and your end user. The end user will determine how technical it is. You may need to install the system for them, if this is the case then the user guide should include where and how it has been installed, for future reference. You may need to set up folders for reports to be saved in or for archiving purposes.

Remember user guides are often one of the first parts of a project that a marker goes to look at as they show very clearly what the student has actually produced, whether it does work, and whether the student really understands it!

Evaluation and report

Evaluation

The criteria that must be met to gain the highest mark band for the evaluation are:

> **'The candidate has considered *clearly* a *full* range of *qualitative* and *quantitative* criteria for evaluating the solution. The candidate has *fully* evaluated his/her solution *intelligently* against the requirements of the user(s). *Evidence of end user involvement during this stage has been provided.'*

The key words have again been italicised to show where the emphasis is.

How good a student's evaluation is depends on several things:

- how good their analysis was,
- whether they have a good understanding of what this system was supposed to achieve,
- how clear their end user requirements are,
- how clear their performance criteria for the solution are,
- whether they have used quantitative performance criteria,
- whether their testing has tested the system produced against the performance criteria and end user requirements,
- whether their end user testing has tested the end user's requirements,
- how much evidence of testing they have,
- whether they have left enough time to do this section!

It would be expected that a student will quote evidence from the report to back up statements in their evaluation and that they will follow the evaluation through methodically and clearly.

Here are some examples of how you can write up your evaluation:

End user requirement: The solution should produce a quotation that is 100% accurate.

This evaluation criterion has been met, at least as far as can be seen from the testing carried out in the time available. When the solution was tested with data sets A and B, the calculations necessary to produce a quotation were checked by using a calculator (see tests 34 and 35). When Mr Green tried out the solution by producing a quotation for a real job, he compared the result he got with his old manual method and said, 'This is going to stop me from making a lot of mistakes, I'd forgotten to add in the transport costs when I did it manually.' (See copy of letter from Mr Green on page 97.)

End user requirement: The web pages should be easy to navigate for all visitors to the site.

This criterion was met as a consistent user interface has been developed for the website. As can be seen on the printouts of web pages on pages 46–54, there is a common nagivation bar which is always situated in the same place on the page, and which has the page that the visitor is currently on highlighted in a different colour. The background page colour corresponds to the colour of the page tab on the navigation bar.

Evidence that this does make navigating the site easier for visitors is shown by the copies of emails received from visitors to the site on pages 67–69. The first two emails are from first time visitors, while the others are from people who have visited the site several times. It can also be seen from their comments that they have visited the site for different reasons and so have needed to navigate to different areas.

End user requirement: Stock levels should be adjusted after every order is produced to keep them accurate.

> The solution does not meet this criterion. I had not realised that when people make orders they can sometimes decide part way through that they don't want to continue with the order. This can be either because the company doesn't have all of the products they want in stock, or the price of an item isn't good enough. It can even happen at the end of recording an order when the customer finds out he can't get a discount! This problem only appeared when my end user was trying the solution out in his office and he checked the stock levels after he had had one of these cancelled orders and realised it didn't work properly. His comments are shown on page 87.

Remember, the evaluation is an evaluation of the solution that you have produced. It is not an evaluation of you or your knowledge, or your teacher's knowledge. It must be objective and factual with proof provided to back up the statements you make. All of the examples shown above have evidence quoted in them.

Limitations of the system produced must be included – these are the things that don't work as they should – where the system has failed to meet the evaluation criteria and requirements.

Enhancements are what can be done to improve the system. These are the sort of thing that crops up when the end user says 'Oh I didn't know you could do that, I would like to produce emails to suppliers with orders in'. End users' views of what they require frequently change over the development time of a system, the longer the development time the worse this problem is – in some cases staff change and the new staff have totally different ideas to the old ones. Hopefully you won't get this problem when you do your projects!

Above all be honest in the evaluation – don't pretend things work if they don't or you have failed to provide evidence that they do.

If you have spent the time in the earlier stages this section should be straightforward to complete and should help to boost your marks!

Preparation of the report

'A *well* written, *fully* illustrated and *organised* report has been produced. It describes the project *accurately* and *concisely*.'

If you adopt the approaches described in this book then you should be able to produce a report that meets these criteria. The key points that a marker will be looking for are:

1 Is the project easy to find your way around?
2 Does it have a list of contents and page numbers?
3 Are diagrams numbered and titled? Do printouts etc. have headings?
4 Can you easily track a process from analysis through to design, to implementation and testing? Is cross-referencing effective?
5 Are all printouts and screenshots fully annotated and are they necessary?
6 Is the project well bound and is it clear to see whom it belongs to and what it is about?

Some things a marker doesn't want to see:

1 Pages of printouts that are unannotated.
2 No contents page.
3 Lots of sample documents just stuck in an appendix – if it is relevant it should be *where* it is relevant, labelled and used.
4 Printouts they can't read.
5 Projects that tell them how to use the software.
6 Projects that have pages and pages of tedious testing of button pressing.
7 Projects that fall apart when you try to mark them.
8 Projects that have no title and they can't tell whose they are.
9 Projects where they have to keep flicking back and forward between appendices and the body of the report.
10 Projects where the student hasn't even used a spell checker.
11 Projects where a fancy font has been used which makes it harder to read.

12 Projects where the student has wasted time on unimportant elements – like using software to produce data flow diagrams.

13 Projects where the student has ignored their teacher's advice.

14 Evidence of end user involvement that isn't genuine.

15 Projects where the student has run out of time and lost a lot of marks.

16 Projects that have been copied from text books or where students have failed to admit to help they have received or bits of pre-written code they have used.

17 Projects where you can tell the student has produced a good system but they have lost marks because they haven't done the documentation.

18 The student that has nearly full marks on implementation and virtually no marks for analysis or design.

19 Projects that have failed because a wrong choice of system was made to begin with, for example one that was too large or too small.

20 Projects that have failed because the student didn't understand what they were doing and probably never asked for help.

21 Projects that are too big – quantity does not necessarily mean quality in project work!

If you can avoid all of these then you should have a good report and a good project!

Final tips

How to submit your project work and final reminders

This is really a quick check list for you to follow to make sure that what you hand in is easy to mark – if it is then the marker will be able to find the evidence more easily to be able to award you the marks that you deserve!

1   Keep to deadlines set by your teachers. These are usually planned so that they can give you feedback and allow you to improve your work.

2   Use techniques to cut down on the amount of printouts and paperwork that you need to include – follow the tips in this and the AS book.

3   Make sure that you have a copy of the marking criteria used to assess your project work. There may be other guidance notes from the specification that you can use. Specifications are published on examination board websites.

4   Check that you have met all of the criteria to the best of your ability in the time available.

5   Don't leave anything out that might be useful.

6   Bind your project well so that pages don't fall out. Some exam boards will not let you use hard backed folders and you certainly shouldn't use plastic wallets for each individual sheet.

7   Do make sure that your user guide is securely fastened in to the project report.

8   Spiral binding with a piece of card at the front and back is probably the best way to bind the project.

9   Make sure the project is labelled with your name, candidate number, centre number, unit entered for and a title.

10 Have a list of contents and use page numbers.

11 Avoid the use of appendices, if it's relevant put it where it is needed – this applies for example, to designs, sample documents, printouts.

12 Use a spell checker and a grammar checker or get someone else to read the project and check it for errors.

13 Listen to comments your teacher makes and act on them.

14 Don't leave pencil comments by your teacher telling you to put something else in or change something, on your work.

15 Do make sure that someone can read your printouts without a magnifying glass.

16 Do admit to any help or materials that you have used.

17 Don't think that you can finish a project in a weekend and get a good mark.

18 Do remember that marks gained on projects count towards your overall grade. Sometimes one mark on a project is worth two in an exam – in other words poor project work means a poor overall grade.

19 You have control over the project work, you don't write the exam questions.

20 Enjoy it – luckily project work in ICT is more like the real world than probably most other work that you will be doing!